The Story of Zacchaeus
A Rap

Written by John Kivell

Copyright © 2015 John Kivell.

All rights reserved. No part of this book may be used or reproduced by any means, graphic, electronic, or mechanical, including photocopying, recording, taping or by any information storage retrieval system without the written permission of the publisher except in the case of brief quotations embodied in critical articles and reviews.

WestBow Press books may be ordered through booksellers or by contacting:

WestBow Press
A Division of Thomas Nelson & Zondervan
1663 Liberty Drive
Bloomington, IN 47403
www.westbowpress.com
1 (866) 928-1240

Because of the dynamic nature of the Internet, any web addresses or links contained in this book may have changed since publication and may no longer be valid. The views expressed in this work are solely those of the author and do not necessarily reflect the views of the publisher, and the publisher hereby disclaims any responsibility for them.

Any people depicted in stock imagery provided by Thinkstock are models, and such images are being used for illustrative purposes only.
Certain stock imagery © Thinkstock.

ISBN: 978-1-4908-7195-0 (sc)
ISBN: 978-1-4908-7194-3 (e)

Library of Congress Control Number: 2015903424

Print information available on the last page.

WestBow Press rev. date: 3/16/2015

The Story of Zacchaeus
A Rap

To present this story as a rap, have your audience do a rhythm by slapping their thighs twice, then clapping once.

Eg: thigh, thigh, clap… thigh, thigh, clap… etc.

Now here's a little tale about a guy named Zacchaeus

A short little dude, even shorter than (he/she) is*

He was a tax collector, not a popular guy

He didn't have a lot of friends; it isn't hard to see why

*Point to the shortest person, if it will not hurt their feelings.

'Cause back in those days when you had to pay your taxes

You couldn't mail 'em in, you couldn't send them by fax. As…

…a matter of fact there was only one way;

A guy like Zacchaeus is who you had to pay.

And sometimes he would take more than his share.

Now it wasn't very honest but he didn't really care

'Cause that's the way it had always been done

And Zacchaeus said, "Change? Why should I be the one?"

"Everybody does it, so what's the big deal

If I tell a little lie, or if I cheat, or if I steal?"

Now you or I wouldn't behave that way

But Zacchaeus didn't care…

…He did it anyway.

Now Jesus came to town on a cross-country tour

He was healing the sick, he was preachin' to the poor

He was spreadin' good news all across the land

Talkin' in a way that we all can understand

About God, the Father, and His love for everyone.

You see, God was Jesus' father, and he was God's Son

Now wherever Jesus went there was a real big crowd,

People pushing, people shoving, people shouting real loud.

Zacchaeus came along and he wanted to find out

What all the fussin' and commotion was about,

So he climbed up to the top of a sycamore tree.

(Remember, he was short. It was the only way to see)…

Well, Jesus came along and he looked up in the tree

And he saw Zacchaeus sittin' there, plain as could be,

And Jesus said, "Zacchaeus!"

Zacchaeus said, "Me?"

Jesus said, "Yes you, get out of that tree,"

"Come down here, I want to talk to you."

He said, "I'm coming to your house about half past two."

So Zacchaeus went home, and Jesus came along.

They talked a little while, Zacchaeus saw where he was wrong

He said, "Forgive me, Lord, I`ll give half of everything

That I own to the poor, and another thing,

I`ll pay everyone I stole from four times back,

And I`ll be a good boy, or my name`s not Zack!"

And Jesus said, "Hey Zacchaeus, that's the way!

Salvation has come to your house today!"

Well, this all happened a long time ago

Zacchaeus isn't here, but this much I know;

Jesus is still with us, I don`t know if the tree is,

But that`s all there is about the guy named Zacchaeus.

Bomp Bomp

Diddely

Bomp de

Bomp Bomp

(Be sure to read the real story of Zacchaeus in your own Bible in Luke chapter 19.)

Remember that if you have asked Jesus into your heart, he will be your friend forever. Even if you do something you know is wrong, he will still love you. You just need to say to him, "Jesus, I'm sorry" and he will forgive you and give you a fresh start all over again.

CPSIA information can be obtained at www.ICGtesting.com
Printed in the USA
LVOW02s1901050415

433296LV00004B/11/P